William the Conqueror

JUNIOR HISTORIES

Series Editor Alain Plessis

WILLIAM THE CONQUEROR

Philippe Brochard

Illustrated by Pierre Brochard

Hart-Davis

Pirates from the North

In the eighth century, many countries in western Europe were invaded by new groups of people who attacked them from all directions. The Saxons, the Hungarians and the Bulgarians advanced from the east, while the Arabs moved up from the south. At first, the people living in the north of Europe seemed to have escaped. One day, however, without warning, people who lived along the coasts of Scotland and England were terrified by the sight of wild and savage men pouring out of strange-looking ships. These men were pirates, who continued to move inland, massacring those in their path, plundering the rich abbeys in lonely places, destroying villages, and carrying men and women away into slavery. For two hundred years, they spread fear wherever they went. Their helpless victims could only pray that God would 'deliver them from the fury of the Northmen'. They did not know that these pirates came from a highly developed society of people living around the **fjords** of **Scandinavia.** Some of these Northmen were farmers who lived in comfortable wooden houses. Others were craftsmen who loved precious objects and fine fabrics, merchants who lived in trading towns or sailors who were brave enough to set sail on the wild northern seas. They were not Christians but believed in a number of gods, the most important of whom were **Thor** and **Odin**. These Northmen were known as Vikings.

Fjord
A long narrow arm of the sea stretching inland between steep cliffs or mountains, common along the Norwegian coast.

Scandinavia
The name given to an area of North West Europe, made up of Denmark, Norway, Finland and Sweden.

Thor and Odin
Scandinavian gods. Odin was the father of all the gods and Thor his son was the god of thunder and lightning.

ATLANTIC

VIKINGS

OCEAN

MEDITERRANEAN S.

0   1 000 km

Viking Ships
The Vikings went to sea in all weather conditions. They often placed the carved wooden head of an animal at the prow of the boat. For this reason a boat could be known as a snekkar, (the head of a serpent) or a drakkar (the head of a dragon). Their boats were equipped with both oars and sails

Vikings or Normans?

Countries along the coast or near to the rivers were easy prey for men as skilled in navigation as the Vikings. Groups of Vikings attacked Scotland and Ireland, placed a large part of England under **Danelaw** and forced the English to pay **tribute**. Others moved along the River Elbe and sacked Hamburg. They sailed up the River Rhine and burnt Mayence. They took over the Seine Valley and beseiged Paris. Viking camps were established everywhere: along the Loire, the Meuse and the Garonne for example. From these bases they launched other expeditions. The king of France, Charles III, whose nickname was Charles the Simple, was not strong enough to stop them. He made a treaty in 911 with one of their Chieftains called Rolf or Rollo. Charles agreed that Rollo should rule **Neustria** in return for a promise of peace. Rollo and his followers became settlers rather than pirates, anxious to defend their own land. Other groups of Vikings continued to spread throughout Europe. The **Varangians** imposed their law on the Slav peoples and founded **Russia**. The Norwegians settled in Iceland, then in Greenland. One of them, Leif, the son of Eric the Red, discovered land which he called **Vinland**. This was probably part of America.

Danelaw
'The law of the Danes'. This word came to describe a region of England which was controlled by the Viking invaders.

Tribute
A tax which is imposed after a battle by the winning side on those they have conquered.

Neustria
The latin name given to the lands situated between the River Seine, the River Loire, Brittany and the Channel, now known as Normandy.

Varangians
The name given to the Swedish Vikings by the Eastern Europeans.

Russia
The Slav peoples called the Viking invaders 'Rus' which is why their country became known as Russia.

Vinland
This word means literally 'the land of the vine'. Historians think that the name refers to the Saint Laurence region in Canada, but, in spite of much research, no one is certain.

Fleeing from the Vikings
The monks of the abbey of Noirmoutier fled because of repeated Viking attacks. They saved what treasures they could and carried with them the casket containing the precious relics of Saint Philibert. They went as far as Burgundy before they felt safe from attack

Robert the Devil

Duchy
Territory governed by a Duke.

Tanner
A tanner treats or 'cures' animal skins so that they can be used to make goods or clothing.

Under its new master, Rollo, Normandy became a **Duchy** and almost independent of the King of France. The first Dukes rebuilt the towns and abbeys like the famous Mont St Michael and reconstructed the parts which had been destroyed. They kept order and re-established justice. Law and order in Normandy was proverbial. The story is told of how the Duke left a gold chain in a tree and was able to collect it three years later from where it still hung in the same place. Rollo's son was called William Long-Sword. His grandson, Robert, was a violent and impetuous man and made himself many enemies. In later times he was given the nickname Robert the Devil. As a young man however he was handsome and charming. One day he fell in love with Herleva the daughter of a **tanner**. Some time afterwards she had a son, William. Later, filled with remorse for all his past sins, Robert decided to go on a pilgrimage to Jerusalem. He named his son William as his heir, in case some ill fortune happened to him on his journey. While on pilgrimage he deliberately attracted attention to himself by behaving with tremendous generosity. Because of this the people who watched him pass called him Robert the Magnificent.

The Byzantine Emperor Constantinople was the capital of his empire

Robert enters Constantinople
Before he entered the city, Robert ordered his mules to be shod with very short golden nails so that they fell out as his baggage train advanced. The Normans then left the nails lying in the roadway in order to make it clear to the bystanders that riches were not important to them

William as a Boy

Vassal
A lord who owed obedience to another more powerful than himself like a Duke or King.

Tutor
A person in charge of educating a child.

Suddenly news came from abroad that Duke Robert, at the early age of twenty five, was dead. His son, William, was still only seven years old. Worse still, William was not Robert's legitimate son because Robert had never actually married William's mother, Herleva. Robert had made the Norman barons, his **vassals**, swear to be loyal to his son but they took advantage of William's youth and broke out in revolt. They were, after all, descended from pirates. One of their number, a captain, Roger de Tosny, had gained a sinister reputation while fighting the Muslims in Spain. It was rumoured that he had ordered the head of an infidel to be served for lunch! Knowing that he no longer had a lord who could punish him, he attacked his neighbour's lands. Some of the other barons followed his example. Private wars broke out all over Normandy. It was an unhappy and very violent time. The young William saw his councillors, his **tutor** and his guardian assassinated one by one. Hevleva's brother had to protect his nephew, so he entrusted him to a simple peasant family, with whom William lived in secret.

A Norman lord

William and the peasant family
William was sheltered for a time by people who had no idea who he really was. Later, William never forgot the ordinary people to whom he owed his life

Saved by a Jester

Court Jester
A Jester, sometimes called a Fool, was a person kept at court by a king or lord to entertain him.

Feudal oath
A feudal oath was the oath sworn to the king, or a great landowner like the Duke, by his lords. They had to swear to be loyal to him and to fight for him in time of war.

At fourteen, William was old enough to take responsibility for his own affairs. Taking no notice of his councillors who were advising him not to act rashly, he made up his mind to recapture his own country. This is what the most educated men of the day: the monks, had advised him to do. The rebellious barons were, however, anxious to make an end of William once and for all. Urged on by Guy of Burgundy, William's cousin, they all met together at Bayeux to lay a trap for the Duke and kill him. The story goes that the **Court Jester** came across the conspirators while they were plotting their treachery. The barons took no notice of him for, they thought, he was only the Fool and not important. As soon as night came, however, the Jester fled and ran to warn the Duke. 'You must escape at once, William, or you will be cut to pieces.' William leapt from bed, saddled a horse and galloped away. In the darkness he heard a band of horsemen coming after him, so he hid behind a hedge. His pursuers did not see him. By the next day William's horse was exhausted and he was completely lost. An elderly knight recognised him and, loyal to his **feudal oath**, gave William shelter and a guide to lead him to his castle at Falaise. When the soldiers who were chasing William arrived, the knight sent them off in the wrong direction. William was safe but for how long?

The Court Jester in the middle ages was often a dwarf

William escapes
William scarcely had time to throw on a few clothes before escaping into the night. Hiding behind a hedge he watched the soldiers searching for him

Duke of Normandy

Capetian monarchy
Since 987 France had been
governed by a line of kings who
were originally descended from
Hugh Capet. The Capetian kings,
as they were called, ruled until 1328.

Besiege
William used all the standard
military tactics of the time, like
wooden siege towers, to besiege
the castles of his enemies.

Duke William knew that without military support
he was lost. The only person he could turn to was his
feudal lord, the King of France. William asked him
for protection. Henry I, the French king, would in
fact, have been happier to see his dangerous cousin
William disappear from the scene, but he knew that
if he did not carry out his duty as a feudal lord his
other subjects would no longer have any confidence
in him. The **Capetian monarchy** was still very weak
and the Capetian kings were afraid of rebellion. By
this politic move William forced the French king to
involve himself in his affairs, and with his help he
defeated his enemies at Val des-Dunes near Caen.
William drove his cousin, Guy of Burgundy, back to
his castle at Brionne. For three years he **beseiged**
Guy's castle. By the end of that time, the Norman
barons either recognised William's authority by
choice, or because they had been forced to, so
William pardoned all the nobles who had fought
against him. He established a network of friends he
could rely on which gave him the confidence to face
another rebellion, when it occurred, and many
enemies outside Normandy. By the middle of the
eleventh century Normandy was, together with
Flanders, the most powerful country within the
Kingdom of France.

A siege tower

The battle of Val des-Dunes
*At Val des-Dunes, William, who
was just twenty, showed great
courage. The King of France, who
fought by his side, was thrown
from the saddle on two occasions*

William's Normandy

The Normans had inherited a deep knowledge of navigation and trade from their Viking ancestors. Drakkars were warships, but many smaller ships, with curved and hollow hulls, were used to carry goods.

Shipwrights applied the same methods they used in ship building to build houses of wooden timbers.

River water was harnessed to power mills and thus provided taxes for the lord or abbot who owned them.

The countryside of Normandy was then planted with vines. It was much later, in the sixteenth century, that the famous Normandy apples were first grown.

The Norman Dukes encouraged trade. Towns and cities grew up and laws were passed which gave the townsmen special privileges.

Hunters tracked down the wild animals in the great forests for meat and fur. The peasants, however, cut down the trees and burnt the undergrowth. The forest clearings made in this way could then be ploughed and crops grown.

The Truce of God

Truce of God
A period of time during which people engaged in warfare would be ordered to stop fighting. The idea of such a Truce was first developed and imposed by the Church.

Monastic schools
The monasteries did not only train monks. Ordinary lay people could send their sons there to be educated.

Abbeys
These were religious foundations. In Greek the word Abba means father, so the head of all the monks was called the Abbot, or father.

Excommunicated
A man is excommunicated when the Church, because his actions are considered to be so grave and sinful, decides to pronounce the ban of excommunication against him. The excommunicated person is not allowed to take part in any Church services, or attend Mass. While the Duke was excommunicated, all the Norman churches were closed.

In 1049, the Pope announced the **Truce of God**. William seized eagerly on this idea and used it to his own advantage. He ordered his lords not to fight during the period from Easter to Whitsun and all the year round from Friday night to Monday morning. Of course, in a world used to violent crimes and private wars, this order was not easy to enforce. William, therefore, relied on the moral authority of the monks. He summoned people who had been pupils in the famous **monastic schools** of Burgundy and Italy. They were ordered to refound and rebuild the Norman **abbeys**. The abbeys at Fécamp and Bec were to serve as models for the rest. At this time, a monastery was not only a place of prayer. The monks taught many pupils to read and write and they copied ancient texts. William knew that he had to educate men to accept the Truce rather than impose it on them by force. Then, in 1049, William, who had done so much for the Church, was **excommunicated**. The problem was that William wanted to marry Matilda, daughter of the Count of Flanders. The Pope insisted that Matilda and William were cousins and that the marriage was therefore impossible. William ignored him and married Matilda in 1053. But the Duchy of Normandy remained under the ban of excommunication for ten years.

The building of the Abbey of Bec
William hoped that the important people of his duchy would be educated in the abbeys. The Italian monk Lanfranc, a close friend of William, made the abbey of Bec a famous centre of learning. Lanfranc also tried to persuade the Pope to lift the ban of excommunication from William

Order and Justice

Homage
This is the act by which a man was recognized as a vassal by his lord. The vassal knelt in front of his lord and placed his hands inside his lords hands.

Fief
Land granted by a lord to his vassal.

Felon
A traitor who did not remain loyal to his lord.

Normandy was controlled by lords whose authority was structured rather like a pyramid. At the top was the Duke. William had learnt while he was still very young not to trust other men so he did not delegate any of his power. All final decisions were his. His power was absolute and centralized. He relied on his barons to help him administer the Duchy. Three times a year he called his council together in order to discuss important matters with the powerful lords or to dispense justice. He received the **homage** of his vassals and, in exchange gave them lands which became their **fief**. These powerful vassals were expected to impose justice within their fiefs, and defend their Duke in time of war. Around this time, the Norman lords began to build the new stone castles, which later were to grow in size and became more like fortresses. William did not wholly approve of these buildings, where rebellious lords, or **felons**, could easily take refuge. This is why he appointed loyal and trustworthy people as governors of these castles. He also kept the largest army in France and could protect the Duchy against his neighbours: the Bretons, the Angevins and the friends of the King of France. Henry I was now his enemy but William was able to defeat him on two occasions.

A Norman knight in armour

The first wooden castles
The first step was the construction of the motte, or mound. The workmen dug a circular ditch which they then fortified. They then threw all the earth which they had dug out of the ditch into the centre to make a mound. On this they built a wooden tower. Later these were replaced with strong stone keeps

The Norman Invasion

William had other ambitions. Across the channel, England, torn apart by wars, was a tempting prey. The **Anglo-Saxons** had been fighting Danish invaders for more than two hundred years. The English King Edward was a man who was highly respected for his wisdom and was known as Edward the Confessor because of the support he had given to the Church. His mother came from Normandy and spoke French. Edward had surrounded himself with Norman guards and it seems likely, because he was childless, that he had promised William he would succeed him as king. By the closing years of Edward's reign, however, the most powerful man in England was the ambitious Earl Harold of Wessex. In 1064 Harold set sail for Normandy, on a mission for King Edward, but his ship was blown off course. He was seized and eventually brought to William's court, where the story goes that he promised to be William's vassal and support him in his claim to the English throne. However, when Edward died, Harold had himself crowned King of England. William decided to claim the English throne by force. He had many lords and knights willing to join him in this enterprise in order to win fame and lands for themselves. Two Norman knights had already conquered Sicily and Southern Italy. William had a huge fleet constructed which he loaded with weapons, horses and supplies. By September everything was ready and the Duke waited for a favourable wind so that he could sail across the channel.

Edward the Confessor

William leaves for England
The invasion fleet assembled on the beach at Dives in Normandy. In all, there were probably about two thousand ships

God to our Aid!

At last the wind changed and the Normans landed on English soil. King Harold was still in the north of England where he had just defeated a Viking invasion force at the Battle of Stamford Bridge. He made a forced march with his companions towards the south coast where he took up his position on the side of a hill near the village of Hastings facing the Norman invaders. He arranged his men in tightly packed ranks to make a human barrier. In front he put his famous **axe men**. William was relying on his cavalry and ordered them to advance several times. Each time the Norman cavalry was driven back, men fell from their horses, and hand to hand fighting broke out. For a moment the Normans believed that William had been killed and panic quickly spread throughout the Norman camp. The Duke had to take off his helmet and show his face to his men to quell their fears. Seeing that he would never be able to break through the wall of human beings, William ordered the Normans to pretend to flee. Harold's army ran down the hill in pursuit but then the Norman cavalry turned and rode back dispersing the Anglo-Saxons and killing a great number of them. Finally, William ordered his archers to shoot in the air. An arrow pierced Harold in the eye and killed him. His men lost heart and fled away. By the evening it was clear that William had won the battle. Now he would be known as 'William the Conqueror'.

God to our aid!
This was what the Normans shouted as they swept into battle. The Viking would shout 'Thor aid us!' but the Normans had christianized this ancient war cry.

Axe men
These were the élite of Harold's army. The only weapon they carried was a razor sharp axe. They boasted that they could cut off the head of a horse with a single blow.

An axeman with his axe

The confusion of battle
Soldiers did not wear special uniform in the middle ages. Sometimes it was very difficult to see whose side they were on. William had to take off his helmet in order to prove to his soldiers that he was still alive

A Record of Events:

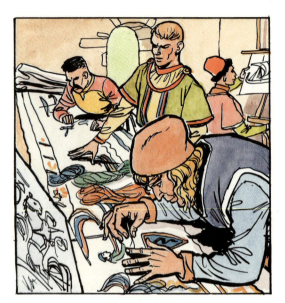

William ordered Anglo-Saxon craftsmen to embroider a record of the events of the Conquest in wool on a long strip of linen.

The tapestry tells us a great deal about the lives of people at that time for many details of everyday life are shown in the embroidery.

At first the tapestry probably adorned the inside of the Cathedral of Bayeux. It was about 70 metres long and 50cm wide. During the French Revolution it was forgotten but Napoleon used it as a means of propaganda against the British at a time when he also was thinking of invading Britain.

The Bayeux Tapestry

The tapestry consists of over 70 scenes, among them Harold's visit to Normandy, Edward's death, and William's preparations for the invasion, with a running text in Latin. The scenes are beautifully drawn and skilfully embroidered. It was a magnificent work of propaganda thought up by William to justify his invasion.

The Domesday Book

Thegn
An Anglo-Saxon lord.

Pacification
The process by which peace is established throughout a country.

The day after the battle, the Normans began to extend their control over southern England. Once he had secured London, William decided to have himself crowned king as soon as possible. The ceremony was held in Westminster Abbey on Christmas Day, 1066. The powerful Anglo-Saxon **thegns** swore to be loyal to William but soon he had to face many rebels, Anglo-Saxon, Scandinavian, and French, including his own son who tried to seize power in Normandy. The **pacification** of England lasted six years. One of the last rebel groups, headed by Hereward the Wake held out in the marshes of East Anglia for some time. William, old by now, and grown weary of rebellion, showed little mercy to the Anglo-Saxons. He confiscated the lands of the thegns and distributed them amongst his Norman followers. In order to do this fairly, and in order that he would know exactly what kind of land he had conquered, what it produced and how much it was worth, he ordered a survey of the whole country to be made. All the information was collected into a large volume which came to be called the 'Domesday Book' or the Book of the Last Judgement. William kept strict control over his lands until the end. He died, worn out, at Rouen, in 1087, when he was fifty nine years old.

A Saxon thegn

The Domesday Survey
William's officials listed all the lands and valuable things like ploughs, oxen, forests, mills and dwellings belonging to the deposed Anglo-Saxon thegns

Norman England

Following the Conquest, England became drawn into life on the Continent of Europe. Normandy and England had especially close ties.

For a long time the Anglo-Saxons were bitter at being defeated. Some would not accept Norman rule and fled to the forests where they became outlaws.

The ruling classes were Norman. The ordinary people remained Anglo-Saxon. Each spoke a different language. A lord, for example would speak of 'un mouton' or 'un porc' while a peasant would still speak of 'a sheep' or 'a pig'. The difference still remains today in English when we speak of the meat of an animal (mutton or pork) or of the animal itself.

IRELAND

THE
PRINCIPALITY
OF WALES

York

THE KINGDOM
OF ENGLAND

Thames   London
Windsor

Hastings

THE CHANNEL

Flanders

THE GERMAN EMPIRE

Rhine

Rouen
Bayeux   Caen   Saint-Clair-sur-Epte
The Duchy   Paris
of Normandy   Champagne

Brittany   Maine
                    Orleans

THE ATLANTIC   Anjou
                     Angers   Chinon   The Duchy
OCEAN   of
                                              Burgundy
              Poitou
                         Marche

              La Rochelle

                                     Auvergne

                        Bordeaux
                        Garonne

0   200 km
                   Aquitaine   Toulouse
                   Bayonne   THE

Rhône

Loire

■ Lands of the French king
■ Lands of the French king's vassals
■ Possessions of the English king
   at the end of the 12th century

MEDITERRANEAN
SEA

England rapidly grew powerful. William's grand-daughter married the Duke of
Anjou. She became the sole heir to both England and Normandy. Her son married
the Duchess of Aquitaine. Because of these two marriages, the English king
possessed half of the Kingdom of France. This was the reason for the many
conflicts between the two countries in the Middle Ages.

First published in Great Britain 1982 by
Hart-Davis Educational Ltd, Frogmore, St Albans
Hertfordshire

Copyright © Hart-Davis Educational Ltd 1982 for
this translation
Translated and adapted by Merle Philo

ISBN 0 247 13226 8

Copyright © Hachette, Paris 1980 for original
French Edition

Granada ®
Granada Publishing ®

Set in England by Martins Press Ltd.
Printed and bound in Great Britain by
William Clowes (Beccles) Limited,
Beccles and London

© Hachette 1980